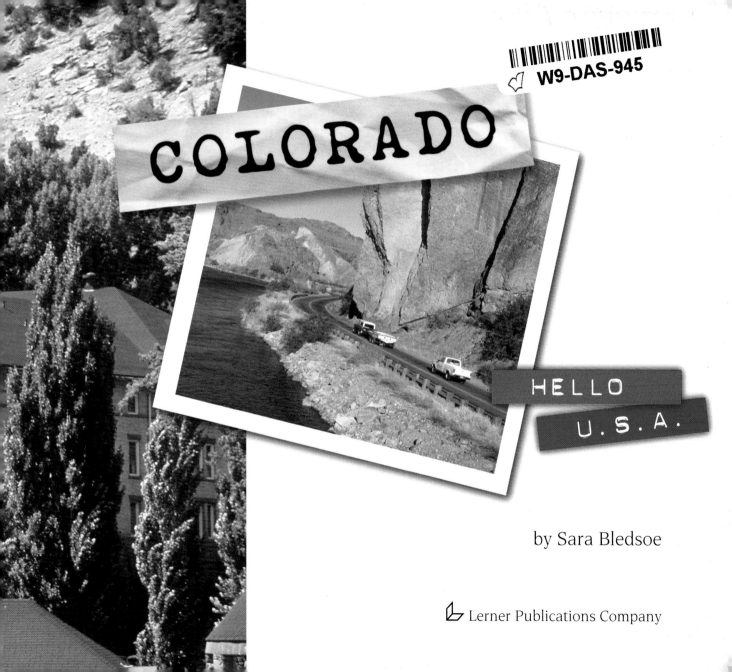

COLORADO

HELLO
U.S.A.

by Sara Bledsoe

Lerner Publications Company

You'll find this picture of wildflowers in Colorado's Roosevelt National Forest at the beginning of every chapter in this book. The foothills of the Rocky Mountains are often covered with a blanket of hardy flowers in the early spring.

Cover (left): A skier in the Arapahoe Basin. Cover (right): Colorado State Capitol. Pages 2–3: Rooftops in Glenwood Springs. Page 3: The Colorado River.

This book is available in two editions:
Library binding by Lerner Publications Company, a division of Lerner Publishing Group
Soft cover by First Avenue Editions, an imprint of Lerner Publishing Group
241 First Avenue North
Minneapolis, MN 55401 U.S.A.

Website address: www.lernerbooks.com

Library of Congress Cataloging-in-Publication Data

Bledsoe, Sara.
    Colorado / by Sara Bledsoe. (Rev. & expanded 2nd ed.)
      p.   cm. — (Hello U.S.A.)
    Includes index.
    ISBN: 0–8225–4055–X (lib. bdg. : alk. paper)
    ISBN: 0–8225–4153–X (pbk. : alk. paper)
    1. Colorado—Juvenile literature. [1. Colorado.] I. Title. II. Series.
  F776.3 .B58 2002
  978.8—dc21   2001000328

Manufactured in the United States of America
1 2 3 4 5 6 – JR – 07 06 05 04 03 02

COLORADO

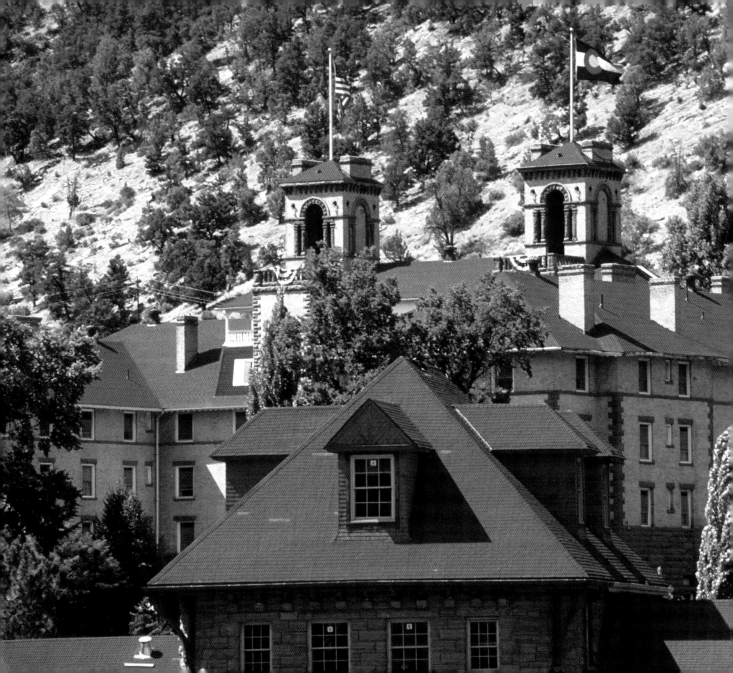

CONTENTS

Mount Elbert pierces the sky near Leadville, Colorado. At 14,433 feet, it is the highest peak in the entire Rocky Mountain system.

THE LAND

The Roof of North America

olorado's claim to fame is not that it's the biggest, the smallest, or even the most populated state in the nation. Colorado, sometimes called the Roof of North America, is the tallest state!

With more than 50 peaks reaching above 14,000 feet, Colorado can boast about having the highest mountains in the United States. These rugged peaks are part of the Rocky Mountains, a long chain of mountains that runs north to south from Canada to New Mexico.

Colorado, a Rocky Mountain state, is bordered by New Mexico, Arizona, Utah, Wyoming, Nebraska, Kansas, and Oklahoma. The Rocky Mountains (also called the Rockies) are probably the best-known feature of Colorado.

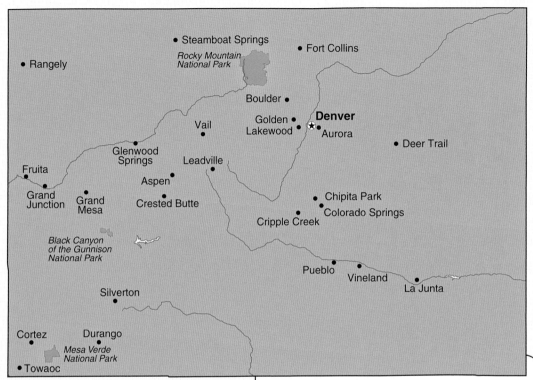

- Rangely
- Steamboat Springs

Rocky Mountain
National Park

- Fort Collins

- Boulder

Vail

- Golden
- Lakewood

Denver
- Aurora

- Deer Trail

Glenwood
Springs

Leadville

Fruita

- Aspen

Grand
Junction

Grand
Mesa

Crested Butte

- Chipita Park
- Colorado Springs

Cripple Creek

Black Canyon
of the Gunnison
National Park

- Pueblo
- Vineland

La Junta

Silverton

Cortez

Durango

Mesa Verde
National Park

- Towaoc

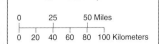

COLORADO
Political Map

★ State capital

0   25   50 Miles

0   20   40   60   80   100 Kilometers

The drawing of Colorado on this page
is called a political map. It shows features
created by people, including cities,
railways, and parks. The map on the
facing page is called a physical map. It
shows physical features of Colorado,
such as coasts, islands, mountains,
rivers, and lakes. The colors represent a
range of elevations, or heights above sea
level (see legend box). This map also
shows the geographical regions of Colorado.

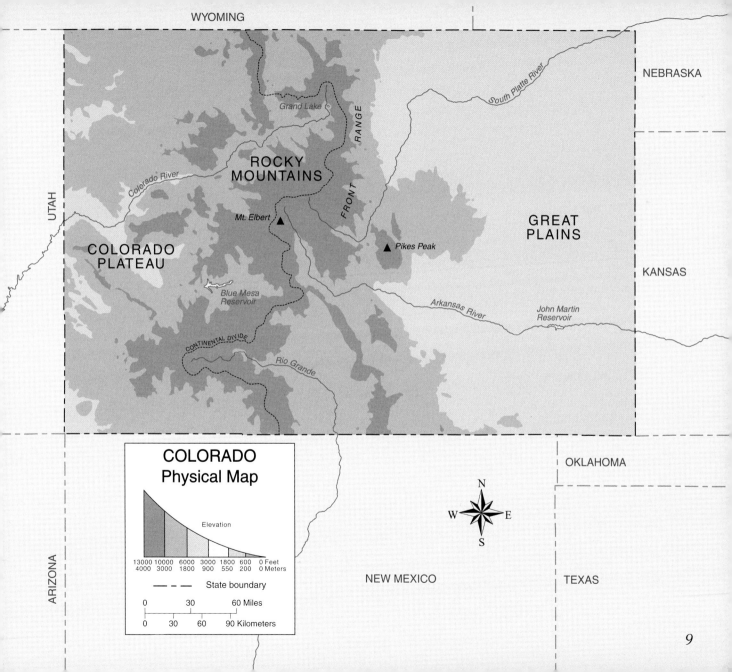

WYOMING

NEBRASKA

UTAH

Grand Lake

ROCKY MOUNTAINS

Colorado River

FRONT RANGE

Mt. Elbert ▲

South Platte River

GREAT PLAINS

COLORADO PLATEAU

▲ *Pikes Peak*

KANSAS

Blue Mesa Reservoir

CONTINENTAL DIVIDE

Arkansas River

John Martin Reservoir

Rio Grande

COLORADO
Physical Map

Elevation

| 13000 | 10000 | 6000 | 3000 | 1800 | 600 | 0 Feet |
| 4000 | 3000 | 1800 | 900 | 550 | 200 | 0 Meters |

- - -   State boundary

```
0          30          60 Miles
0     30     60     90 Kilometers
```

N
W   E
S

OKLAHOMA

ARIZONA

NEW MEXICO

TEXAS

A hiker crosses the Continental Divide in Colorado's Rocky Mountain National Park.

The Rocky Mountain region, which covers central Colorado, makes up only about two-fifths of the state. The Great Plains region, which lies east of the Rockies, stretches across another two-fifths of Colorado. The Colorado Plateau covers the remaining one-fifth of the state.

Colorado's Rockies are made up of five mountain ranges. Four **parks,** or high and wide valleys, separate the ranges. The Front Range is the first row of mountains to rise up from the Great Plains in north central Colorado.

Workers have built highways through many of the mountain **passes,** or openings, low in the ranges. The highways have made it easy for people to travel from one part of the state to another, except when the passes are closed because of a severe snowstorm or the threat of an avalanche.

The **Continental Divide** runs along the tops of the Rocky Mountains. The divide separates Colorado's Rockies into sections known as the

Eastern Slope and the Western Slope. Rivers that begin on the Eastern Slope flow toward the Atlantic Ocean. Rivers on the Western Slope flow toward the Pacific Ocean.

Colorado's Great Plains region is part of a vast stretch of flat land that extends from Canada to Texas. Low hills and **bluffs,** or cliffs, occasionally break the land. At the western edge of the plains, a narrow strip at the foot of the Front Range is home to more than 80 percent of Colorado's population. Most of Colorado's farms and ranches are located on the rest of the Great Plains region, much of which is covered with grasses.

Like other **plateaus,** the Colorado Plateau region looks like a high tabletop. It is very hard and rocky. Over thousands of years, rivers rushing down from the mountains have worn through some of the rock, making deep valleys. The rivers have also created **mesas,** or steep-sided hills with flat tops. Throughout the region, gusting winds have carved out huge rock formations that look big enough to have been made by giants.

Strong winds often cut across Colorado's open plains, leaving ridge marks in the snow.

Jagged rock formations jut up from the ground at the Colorado National Monument, on the Colorado Plateau.

Several major rivers flow across Colorado. High in the mountains, the Colorado River begins its westward journey at Grand Lake. The Rio Grande (Spanish for "big river") starts its course in southern Colorado. The South Platte and the Arkansas Rivers race down the Eastern Slope, then flow across the plains.

Coloradans experience all four seasons. But Colorado's weather is unusual because it can change dramatically within short distances. Just 90 miles from a snowstorm in the mountains, for instance, the winter sun might be warming the plains.

January temperatures average 28° F on the Great Plains and 18° F in the mountains. Snowstorms are common in the winter—especially in the mountains, where up to 400 inches a year may fall. But a snowstorm one day is likely to be followed by bright sunshine the next. In fact, Colorado has about 300 days of sunshine a year.

South Platte River

An elk nibbles on the twigs and needles of a frozen tree branch.

A great variety of animals and plants thrive in Colorado. Antelope, kit foxes, ground squirrels, badgers, coyotes, jackrabbits, and several types of snakes—including rattlesnakes—live on the Great Plains. More than 100 different kinds of plants grow on the region's native sod, or grassland. These plants include buffalo grass, wildflowers, cottonwood and yucca trees, and prickly pear cacti.

Ponderosa pines and cedar trees grow on the foothills of the mountains. Trees such as aspen, spruce, and fir grow higher up in the mountains. Mule deer, moose, elks, mountain lions, black bears, and bighorn sheep are also found on the slopes. In northwestern Colorado, wild horses roam the plateau.

Hikers in Colorado may encounter a gnarly pine tree *(left)*, a coyote *(above top)*, and the scarlet paintbrush *(above)*.

Moisture from snow *(right)* and rain bring colorful wildflowers, such as the wild iris *(below)*, in the spring.

Summers can be hot, windy, and dusty on the plains. Sometimes temperatures reach 100° F, causing many Coloradans to head for the mountains. The plains may not receive rain for weeks in the summer. But, like clockwork, thunderstorms develop in the mountains almost every afternoon between the hours of four and six.

THE HISTORY

Natives and Newcomers

 housands of years before Colorado became a state, Native Americans lived on the mountains, mesas, and plains in the area. Skeletons and a few other remains are about the only evidence we have of these ancient people, and so we know very little about how they lived.

Pottery, jewelry, and tools made by later Indians—the Anasazi—have also been discovered in Colorado. The Anasazi, who lived on the Colorado Plateau from about 100 B.C. to A.D. 1300, hunted and planted gardens for food. They wove baskets using straw, vines, rushes, and the sharp, pointed leaves of the yucca plant. Because of this skill, the Anasazi are also known as the Basket Makers.

A huge dinosaur footprint in one of Colorado's coal mines is at least 60 million years old.

Cliff Palace, the largest cliff dwelling at Mesa Verde National Park, contains hundreds of rooms.

Around the year 750, the Anasazi began to construct apartment-like buildings that we call *pueblos*, the Spanish word for "towns." To build the pueblos, the Indians made bricks from clay. Each pueblo had several floors connected by ladders.

Later, the Anasazi built their homes into the sides of cliffs and eventually became known as Cliff Dwellers. Cliff dwellings shielded the Indians from their enemies and from harsh weather.

The Anasazi were creative farmers, too. To water their crops, the Indians dug narrow ditches from rivers and lakes to their gardens. This method, called **irrigation,** allowed water to flow through the channels to keep the crops healthy during the dry summers.

The Anasazi Indians dug canals to channel water to their crops.

In the year 1276, a long **drought** began. No snow, hail, or rain fell in any large amount for about 23 years. The Anasazi abandoned their dying crops and moved farther south.

Around 1500 the Bannock and the Ute Indians journeyed on foot from what became Utah to Colorado's Western Slope. At the same time, the Apache, Comanche, Kiowa, Navajo, and Pawnee were living in southern Colorado. Later, Arapaho and Cheyenne Indians settled on Colorado's plains.

In 1521, south of Colorado in what later became Mexico, Spanish soldiers set up a colony, or settlement, on Indian lands. The colony, called New Spain, and its Indians were ruled by faraway Spain. The Spaniards also tried to control the Indians in the Colorado area, but the Indians defeated the Spanish forces. The Indians were more than willing, however, to trade with the Spaniards. By the late 1600s, Spanish traders were driving mule trains from Santa Fe (in what later became New Mexico) over the Rockies to Indian settlements along the Arkansas River. Later, this route became

Left: The Arapaho were some of the first Indians to trade with the Spaniards on the Great Plains. *Below:* Spanish explorers saw this deep canyon for the first time in 1540.

part of the Santa Fe Trail, which extended to Missouri.

The Spaniards traded goods such as whiskey, rifles, steel needles, and iron pots for furs and hides provided by the Indians. The Spaniards then sold the furs and hides in Europe, making huge profits.

In 1682 René-Robert Cavelier, Sieur de La Salle, a French explorer, claimed a huge chunk of land in central North America for France. He called the region Louisiana. La Salle's Louisiana included what later became eastern Colorado.

Pikes Peak

When a Spaniard named Juan de Ulibari rode across the Rocky Mountains for the first time in 1706, he discovered that the Indians in eastern Colorado had gotten various items from the French. To protect Spanish trade with the Indians, Ulibari promptly claimed Colorado for Spain. Both France and Spain claimed they owned eastern Colorado at the same time!

In the early 1800s, the two countries agreed that France controlled all of Louisiana. But France was involved in a costly war with Great Britain and needed money. To help pay for the war, France sold Louisiana to the United States in 1803. This sale, called the Louisiana Purchase, doubled the size of the United States.

The U.S. government hired an expedition to explore part of the recently purchased land.

Members of the Pike expedition thought that Pikes Peak was too high to climb. Nowadays, thousands of people take a cog railroad to the top each year.

In 1806 Zebulon Pike, a young army lieutenant, led the expedition to the Rocky Mountains in Colorado.

While crossing the Great Plains, Pike saw a majestic peak a hundred miles away. This mountain would later be named Pikes Peak and become one of the best-known landmarks in the United States. Pike then ventured over the Rockies into Spanish territory, where he was captured by Spaniards and jailed for one year before being released.

In 1821 New Spain gained its independence from Spain and became the country of Mexico. Mexico took over the territories Spain had claimed, including what would become western Colorado. Many **Anglos,** or white people of non-Hispanic descent from the United States, moved to the Mexican territories to trade with the people there.

Mexico and the United States disagreed about where the border between the two countries actually lay. To solve the dispute, the United States wanted to buy some of Mexico's territories. When Mexico refused to hear the terms, the United States sent troops across the border, starting the Mexican War (1846–1848). Mexico was easily defeated.

Ute Indians pose for a picture with visitors.

After the war, Mexico was forced to give land that later became California, Nevada, Utah, and parts of Arizona, New Mexico, Wyoming, and Colorado to the United States. More Anglos moved to the new U.S. territory, building settlements on the home-lands of the Indians.

The U.S. government signed **treaties,** or written agreements, with the Indians in the area. The treaties granted the Indians large tracts of land, called **reservations,** on which they were to live undisturbed by Anglo settlers. But before long, trappers and traders broke the treaties by starting to settle on the outskirts of the reservations and once again disturbing the Indians.

In 1858 gold was discovered in mountain streams along the Front Range, triggering the Pikes Peak gold rush. Nearly 50,000 people flooded the area with high hopes of finding gold and making a for-tune. They set up tents or made makeshift homes. Very few gold prospectors became rich by panning for gold. Many people did not find any gold at all, and some nearly starved.

Besides the prospectors, thousands of men and women came with other dreams of how to get rich. They sold food, clothing, whiskey, donkeys, mining equipment, and other supplies to the miners at high prices.

These businesspeople also built hotels, stores, saloons, stables, houses, churches, and schools. In 1860 the city of Denver was established near the gold mines along the Front Range.

"Pikes Peak or Bust" became the slogan for thousands of gold seekers in 1858.

The Sand Creek Massacre

As cattle ranchers settled on the Great Plains in Colorado in the early 1860s, life changed quickly for the Plains Indians. The large herds of livestock ate so much grass that there was little left for the Indians' horses. And many of the new settlers took pleasure in hunting wild buffalo purely for sport. The Arapaho and Cheyenne Indians depended on buffalo for food and many other needs. As the buffalo herds dwindled, the Indians grew angry.

Tensions rose between the Indians and the settlers, and so did violence. Some bands of Indians attacked wagon trains. And U.S. soldiers killed peaceful Indians. Cheyenne leader Black Kettle wanted to keep peace, and the U.S. Army promised him and his people protection from attacks as long as they camped at Fort Lyon. There, Black Kettle and some other Cheyenne were told to move north to Sand Creek, where they would still be safe.

But Colorado's governor had called together a volunteer army regiment to protect settlers from Indians. To prove the need for the regiment, the governor had to use it. So in 1864 he ordered 700 troops, led by Colonel John Chivington, to march to Sand Creek.

At dawn, Chivington commanded his men to attack the sleeping village. As the Cheyenne stumbled out of their lodges, they tried to fight or hide. Two hundred or more were killed. More than half were women and children. The surprise attack became known as the Sand Creek Massacre.

Denver, founded in 1860, quickly became the center of activity along the Front Range.

Before long, not much gold was left to be mined, and the boom came to an end. People left Colorado by the thousands, but the U.S. government wanted them to stay. It forced the Indians to sell large chunks of reservation land. Every interested Anglo family was given 160 acres of the former reservation land for free, as long as the family used it for farming or planting trees.

In 1876 the United States celebrated its centennial anniversary, an event honoring the country's 100th birthday. That same year, Colorado joined the Union as the 38th state and was nicknamed the Centennial State. Denver became the state capital.

Around the same time, the state experienced another mining boom. In 1873 silver was discovered near Leadville. Prospectors flocked to the area, which belonged to Ute Indians. Land-hungry Anglos flooded into the mountains. The Ute's reservations became smaller.

While more people were moving west to mine or to get free land, transportation was improving. The U.S. government gave railroad companies free land on which to build train tracks so that gold, silver, and people could be easily transported to and from Colorado. Later, the railroad companies sold trackside land to settlers, making huge profits.

A gold strike near Cripple Creek in 1893 and a growing coal-mining industry kept miners busy for the rest of the 1800s. As more people made Colorado their home, local farmers and ranchers began to make a good living by supplying potatoes, corn, wheat, and beef to Coloradans. The state no longer relied on shipments of food from other places. By 1910 more Coloradans were working on farms and ranches than in mines.

Miners sometimes panned for gold in mountain streams.

Construction of Colorado's railroads began in the late 1800s.

Silver King and Baby Doe

In the late 1870s, a boom in silver mining made Horace A. W. Tabor a very wealthy man. Tabor—known as the Silver King—and his beautiful wife, Baby Doe *(above left)*, became a symbol of Colorado's mining booms and busts.

With the profits from his Matchless Mine *(above right)* near Leadville, Horace Tabor spent a lot of money buying expensive gifts and building fancy opera halls. But in 1893, a crash in the price of silver made the Tabors' mine worthless. The Tabors were broke.

Without money from the silver mine, the Tabors counted every penny. But before Horace Tabor died in 1899, he told his wife to watch over the mine, assuring her that someday it would make her rich again.

Baby Doe Tabor followed her husband's instructions. For years she lived alone in poverty, in a wooden shack at the mine's entrance. Mrs. Tabor was found—frozen to death—in the shack. Her Matchless Mine never did produce another fortune.

In the early 1900s, miners in Colorado began to depend on another mineral—oil. Large reserves of oil had been discovered in various parts of Colorado, and oil soon replaced gold and silver as the state's most important mineral.

At the same time, the nation was growing dependent on the automobile. Americans wanted to use their cars to see the country. Thousands of vacationers filled their gas tanks with gasoline, some of which had been made from oil drilled in Colorado. Then many headed for the state to view the magnificent scenery.

During World War I (1914–1918), Colorado's farmers grew tons of wheat to help feed U.S. soldiers. During the war, wheat sold for high prices, so farmers took out loans to buy more farmland. When the war ended, the price of wheat fell. Farmers began losing a lot of money on their crops and were unable to pay back their loans.

Oil wells, such as this one in Vineland, popped up all over Colorado in the 1920s.

By the early 1900s, rather than hope for a lucky strike in a gold or silver mine, many Coloradans turned to the more steady job of farming.

Colorado lost tons of topsoil during the dust storms of the mid-1930s.

Colorado's economic troubles grew worse in 1929. That year marked the beginning of the Great Depression, a major slump in the U.S. economy that lasted through the 1930s. Businesses closed down, and many men and women couldn't find new jobs. Agriculture was hurting, too. For example, the price of a cow dropped from $100 to $16.

Bad weather during the depression added to the farmers' problems. High winds and low rainfall caused blinding dust storms that carried away the rich topsoil of the Great Plains. Some of it blew clear to Washington, D.C.! Crops failed, and thousands of people suffered from lung diseases caused by breathing in the dust-filled air.

By the early 1940s, during World War II, thousands of new jobs pulled Colorado out of the depression. Manufacturing boomed in the state. Factory workers made guns, bombs, bullets, and planes for the war effort. In addition, the U.S. government moved many of its office workers from Washington, D.C., to Colorado. Denver soon became known as the Nation's Western Capital.

During World War II, the U.S. government mined uranium on the Colorado Plateau. The metal was then refined at this plant in Grand Junction and used to produce the highly destructive atomic bomb.

News of more government job openings in the 1950s brought thousands of people to the state. With so many more people, the state needed additional supplies of water. The government planned several irrigation projects. Work on the Frying Pan-Arkansas Project, for example, began in the 1960s. The project channeled water from western Colorado to the dry eastern plains.

Another economic boom came to Colorado in the 1970s and early 1980s, when the state began to drill for more oil. Prices for oil were high at the time, and oil companies in the state made a lot of money.

Colorado did not become a world-famous ski resort until the 1960s.

During the 1980s and 1990s, Colorado continued to experience booms and busts. By 1983, 16 skyscrapers had been built in Denver with money earned from oil. But the price of oil dropped in the mid-1980s, ending another boom.

By the mid-1990s, businesses in the state, including high-tech companies, were thriving. Tourists and new residents flocked to Colorado, attracted by the state's snowy peaks and green valleys. Colorado's natural beauty is as attractive as gold once was to the state's early settlers, and residents must try to preserve it to keep their state growing.

The Denver International Airport, which opened in 1995, added 4,000 jobs to the Denver area.

PEOPLE & ECONOMY

Rocky Mountain Life

olorado has changed a lot since the Anasazi first built their pueblos and the miners their temporary one-room shacks. Many more people live in the modern state of Colorado. Between 1990 and 2000, for example, Colorado's population increased by 31 percent, as people moved to the state seeking jobs. In 2000 Colorado's total population was 4.3 million and growing.

Colorado's largest cities are Denver—the capital—Colorado Springs, Aurora, Lakewood, and Fort Collins.

Opposite page: Colorado's snowcapped mountains, rich variety of wildflowers, and unique historical sites attract many new residents.

This resort in Glenwood Springs features a pool fed by hot springwater.

Many Coloradans learn to ski at an early age.

All of these cities are located on a narrow strip of land along the eastern edge of the Front Range, which offers some of the most beautiful scenery in the United States. More than 80 percent of Colorado's population, or more than 3 million people, live along this strip.

About 75 percent of Coloradans are Anglos. Anglos include people whose ancestors came from Great Britain, Russia, Italy, and Germany. **Latinos**, people who either came from or have ancestors from Latin America, are the state's largest minority group. They make up about 17 percent of Colorado's population.

African Americans make up about 4 percent of the population. Many are descendants of black families who moved to Colorado in the late 1800s. In the 1970s, many people from Vietnam came to the United States to escape war in their homeland. Many of these **immigrants** settled in Colorado. About 2 percent of Colorado's people are Asian American.

Less than 1 percent of Coloradans are Native Americans. Some Indians live on the Ute Mountain Reservation or the Southern Ute Reservation in southwestern Colorado.

A Native American boy dances at a powwow, or ceremonial get-together, in Chipita Park, Colorado.

At one time, almost every man in Colorado worked in one of the state's mines. In modern Colorado, only about 1 percent of the state's workforce has jobs in mining. Miners and engineers still look for gold and silver. But coal, natural gas, and oil are the state's chief mineral products.

Oil wells dot Colorado's Great Plains region.

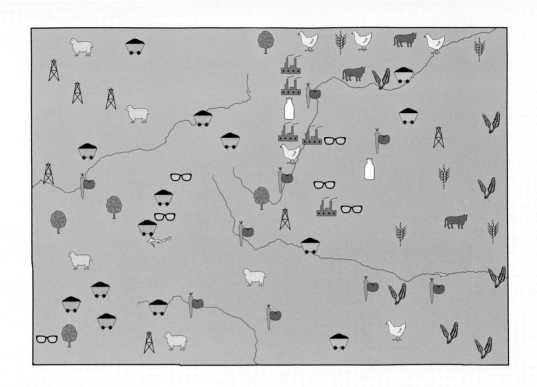

COLORADO
Economic Map

The symbols on this map show where different economic activities take place in Colorado. The legend below explains what each symbol stands for.

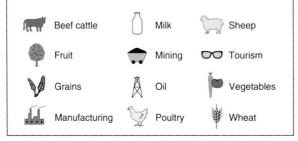

🐄	Beef cattle	🍼	Milk	🐑	Sheep
🍎	Fruit	⛏	Mining	👓	Tourism
🌾	Grains	🗼	Oil	🥕	Vegetables
🏭	Manufacturing	🐓	Poultry	🌾	Wheat

Miners operate huge cranes to dig coal out of the ground. The coal is then shipped in railroad cars to other states, where it is burned as fuel to generate energy for heating and electricity. Natural gas, another source of energy, is sent to other states through underground pipes. Drilling for oil has continued off and on in various parts of the state since the early 1860s.

Ranchers and farmers make up just under 3 percent of Colorado's workforce. Throughout the state, ranchers raise beef cattle. Beef is Colorado's most important agricultural product. Sheep, which are raised for their wool and meat, are herded mainly in the mountains. Farmers on the Great Plains grow wheat, corn, and sugar beets. Cantaloupes are grown along the Arkansas River. On the Colorado Plateau, farmers harvest peaches, apples, and grapes.

Pumpkins are stacked up to be sold at the farmers' market in Boulder, Colorado.

Most of Colorado's cattle graze on the grasses that grow on the Great Plains *(above right)*. Each spring and fall, the animals are rounded up. The calves are branded in spring and weaned and sold in fall *(left)*. Some ranchers raise goats *(above left)*.

Eight percent of Colorado's workers make their living by manufacturing products. Many women and men in Colorado work in factories making computers, medical instruments, cars, planes, skiwear, beer, and suitcases. Colorado's manufactured goods are sold in stores throughout the country. About 7 percent of workers in Colorado have jobs in the construction industry.

About 14 percent of workers in Colorado hold government jobs. These people manufacture coins, maintain national parks and forests, and serve in the U.S. armed forces.

Forest fires sometimes threaten Colorado's wilderness. The services of fire fighters are needed to smother the blazes.

The U.S. government has five military bases in Colorado, as well as the U.S. Air Force Academy, where soldiers train to be air force officers.

The largest number—about 67 percent—of Colorado's workers make their living by providing a wide variety of services. People with service jobs include nurses, pilots, bankers, and store clerks.

Tourism also provides service jobs. More than 25 million people visit Colorado each year for business or pleasure. Service workers provide food, lodging, equipment, and tours to the visitors.

During the winter, vacationers come to Colorado to glide down any of the state's 30 powdery ski slopes. Two of the country's most famous ski resorts are Aspen and Vail, which are open year-round. In the summer, the resorts host conventions. Mountain climbers also come in the summer to scale the highest peaks of the Rockies.

Students at the U.S. Air Force Academy learn to fly military jets.

Hikers in Colorado's Rocky Mountains must be prepared for unexpected snowstorms.

Both tourists and residents delight in Colorado's outdoor wonders. Dinosaur National Monument, Colorado Petrified Forest, Garden of the Gods, and Rocky Mountain National Park are enchanting places to visit. Ancient Anasazi cliff dwellings can be explored at Mesa Verde National Park in southwestern Colorado. In Denver, Six Flags Elitch Gardens and Lakeside Amusement Park offer thrilling rides.

Coloradans enjoy watching professional sports. The Denver Broncos play football at Invesco Field at Mile High, and the Colorado Rockies play baseball at Coors Field. Denver's basketball and ice hockey teams, the Denver Nuggets and the Colorado Avalanche, play their games at the Pepsi Center. Colorado State University, the University of Colorado, and the U.S. Air Force Academy also have popular sports teams.

A Denver Bronco in action

Almost every county in Colorado has a fair and a rodeo. The biggest fair of all, the Colorado State Fair, is held in August and September in Pueblo. Hundreds of people compete for prizes in art, baking, and agriculture. Thousands of visitors enjoy the displays, carnival rides, horse races, rodeos, and musical performances.

A spectacular display of fireworks on New Year's Eve lights up the sky over Pikes Peak.

December and January are special months in Colorado. The Denver City and County Building celebrates the holidays with one of the largest displays of Christmas lights in the nation.

On New Year's Eve in Colorado, the AdAmAn Club (which adds one new member a year) climbs Pikes Peak. At the stroke of midnight, the members set off fireworks, which can be seen on the plains up to 90 miles away. And in mid-January, the National Western Stock Show, complete with professional rodeos, puts on the largest cattle show in the world.

THE ENVIRONMENT

Rare Mountain Air

Cities and towns along Colorado's Front Range continue to grow.

Most Coloradans live in the crowded cities along the Front Range, from Fort Collins in the north to Colorado Springs and Pueblo in the south. The cities and towns along this strip continue to grow. With so many people living and working close together, the Front Range has developed some serious environmental problems. One noticeable problem is smog—a dark, heavy haze in the air.

On some days, a thick smog known as the Brown Cloud hangs over the city of Denver. People with asthma and other lung problems have a hard time

The smoke that pours out of factory smokestacks combines with fog to create smog.

breathing on these days and are advised to stay inside. In addition, the smog smells bad, and the beautiful Rocky Mountains are hidden behind the brown haze.

The word *smog* is actually a blend of two words—"smoke" and "fog." Fog, a thick mist, occurs naturally. But when fog combines with the chemical-filled smoke that pours out of smokestacks at power plants and factories, smog forms.

Factories are responsible for part of the Brown Cloud, but over half of Denver's smog comes from cars, trucks, buses, and planes operating along the Front Range. When these vehicles burn fuel, they release hydrocarbons and nitrogen oxides—chemicals that cling to fog and form smog.

EXIT 213
W 38th Ave
23rd St
EXIT 1/2 MILE

The exhaust from cars and other vehicles on Denver's crowded highways contributes to the Brown Cloud.

The Rocky Mountains worsen Denver's smog problem by acting as a barrier, trapping smog in the area. As more people move to the Front Range, increasing the number of motor vehicles in the region, Denver's Brown Cloud may spread to nearby cities.

When the Denver International Airport opened in 1995, more planes began flying over the Front Range. The new airport has turned Denver into a major stopover between the East and West Coasts.

Airplane traffic over the Front Range has increased since the Denver International Airport opened in 1995.

Buses can carry many people at one time, reducing the number of vehicles on the road and the amount of exhaust in the air.

As a result, people in the Rocky Mountain region have more flights to choose from. The airport has also added jobs, but some people argue that the airplanes have simply added to the smog problem.

Each person in Colorado can help prevent more smog from forming by using motor vehicles less often, an effort that would reduce the amount of chemicals released into the air. To cut down on trips to the mall, people can call ahead to find out if a store carries the product they are looking for. And customers can walk inside fast-food restaurants instead of letting their car engines run while waiting in drive-through lines.

Businesses can encourage employees to share rides to work by offering reduced parking fees for carpoolers. Employers can also sell bus passes at a discount to encourage their workers to take the bus. And, rather than driving or flying to meetings, workers can communicate with customers in other cities by telephone or computer whenever possible.

Residents' efforts paid off in 1990, when Denver won an award for improving its air quality more than any other U.S. city. By 2000 Denver's air quality had met or surpassed federal guidelines for clean air for five years in a row. Much of the change is due to better-running cars and to citizens' reduction of pollution-causing activities. Denver is headed in the right direction toward decreasing its smog.

But many more changes need to be made before the Brown Cloud can disappear. Everyone enjoys breathing good, clean air. Coloradans can preserve and improve their air quality by doing simple activities on a daily basis.

The state government can help by building more walkways and bikeways, so people will have safe places to walk, skate, roller-blade, or bicycle to their destinations. And residents in the Denver area can urge the city to set aside money for rapid transit. Rapid transit systems transport large numbers of people using electric trains, which don't pollute the air as much.

In the meantime, Colorado has required drivers to run their cars through an emissions test every year to see how many hydrocarbons and nitrogen oxides they release. Cars that create too much pollution must be properly tuned up before they can be on the road again legally.

Opposite page: Using bike paths can be both practical and enjoyable.

ALL ABOUT COLORADO

Fun Facts

The highest suspension bridge in the world spans the Royal Gorge, a canyon along the Arkansas River in central Colorado. The river lies 1,053 feet below the bridge.

Boulder, Colorado, is the only U.S. city that gets its water from the melting ice of a glacier. The Arapahoe Glacier, which fills a high mountain valley just northwest of Boulder, supplies the city.

In 1893 Denver, Colorado, became the first major city in the world to grant women the right to vote.

Royal Gorge Suspension Bridge

The state of Colorado takes its name from the Colorado River. Because the river flows through canyons of red stone, early Spanish explorers named the waterway Colorado, which means "colored red."

The 13th stone step outside of the capitol building in Denver, Colorado, is exactly one mile above sea level. In fact, Denver is often called the Mile High City.

Deer Trail, Colorado, was the site of the world's first rodeo. It took place on July 4, 1869.

People in Fruita, Colorado, celebrate "Mike the Headless Chicken Day" in honor of a chicken whose head was cut off in 1945. Farmer L. A. Olsen chopped off the chicken's head only to have Mike live for another 18 months without a head.

Parts of Colorado's Great Plains region receive more hail than any other area in North America.

The worldest largest flattop mountain is in Grand Mesa, Colorado.

STATE SONG

Colorado's state song was officially adopted in 1915. It honors Colorado's state flower and celebrates many of the state's natural features.

WHERE THE COLUMBINES GROW

Words and music by Arthur J. Flynn

'Tis the land where the col - um - bines grow, _____ O - ver -
look - ing the plains far be - low, _____ While the cool sum - mer
breeze in the ev - er - green trees Soft - ly sings where the col - um - bines
grow. _____ Where the scream of the bold moun - tain ea - gle _____ Re -
sponds to the notes of the dove _____ Is the pur - ple robed West, the _____
land that is best. The _____ pi - o - neer land that we love. _____

You can hear "Where the Columbines Grow" by visiting this website:
<http://www.archives.state.co.us/arcembl.html#Song>

A COLORADO RECIPE

In the 1800s, people from all over the world rushed to Colorado to work as loggers, ranchers, and miners. It is said that the Denver Omelette is a result of that mixing of cultures. It may be related to Chinese Egg Foo Yung or a French or Spanish omelette.

DENVER OMELETTE

2 tablespoons butter or margarine
¼ cup chopped onion
¼ cup chopped green pepper
4 eggs
½ cup chopped ham

1. Ask an adult for help with chopping vegetables and ham.
2. In heavy skillet, melt butter or margarine.
3. Add chopped onion and chopped green pepper. Cook over low heat. Stir until onion is tender.
4. Beat eggs. Add chopped ham to eggs.
5. Pour egg mixture into skillet. Cook over low heat until firm. Cut into four wedges and flip over.
6. Remove egg mixture from skillet when slightly brown.

Serves 4.

HISTORICAL TIMELINE

100 B.C.   Anasazi Indians move to the Colorado Plateau.

A.D. 750   Anasazi begin building pueblos.

1276   Drought ruins crops in the Southwest.

1682   René-Robert Cavelier, Sieur de La Salle, claims eastern Colorado for France.

1803   France sells a large portion of land to the United States, including most of Colorado, as part of the Louisiana Purchase.

1806   Zebulon Pike encounters Pikes Peak.

1846   The Mexican War (1846–1848) begins.

1858   The Pikes Peak gold rush attracts thousands of people to Colorado.

1860   The city of Denver is established.

1864   Two hundred Cheyenne men, women, and children are killed in the Sand Creek Massacre.

1873 The discovery of silver near Leadville sets off a silver-mining boom.

1876 Colorado becomes the 38th state.

1893 Denver grants women the right to vote.

1920 Oil becomes Colorado's most important mineral product.

1929 The Great Depression begins, leading to a decline in Colorado's economy.

1941 The United States enters World War II (1939–1945), creating jobs and improving Colorado's economy.

1972 The Frying Pan-Arkansas Project begins operations.

1995 The Denver International Airport opens.

1999 Two students open fire at Columbine High School in Littleton, Colorado, killing 15 people before taking their own lives.

2000 Wildfires in Mesa Verde National Park destroy many of the archaeological artifacts left in the ancient cliff dwellings.

OUTSTANDING COLORADANS

Molly Brown

Scott Carpenter

Kit Carson

Tim Allen (born 1953) is a comedian from Denver, Colorado. Allen's stand-up routine helped him break into television, where he starred in the hit series *Home Improvement*. He has moved on to movies such as *The Santa Clause, Toy Story,* and *Galaxy Quest*.

Margaret ("Molly") Brown (1867–1932) came from a poor family in Missouri before she headed for Leadville, Colorado, where she and her husband, J.J. Brown, made a fortune mining silver. In 1912 Molly sailed on the *Titanic*, a ship that was thought to be unsinkable. When the boat sank, she helped a lifeboat full of people survive the famous wreck. A play and a movie, both entitled *The Unsinkable Molly Brown*, tell the story of Molly's life.

Scott Carpenter (born 1925), from Boulder, Colorado, was one of the first U.S. astronauts in outer space. In 1962 Carpenter and six other Americans orbited Earth three times in the spacecraft *Mercury*.

Christopher ("Kit") Carson (1809–1868) was a trapper, trader, guide, and scout in Colorado and other western territories. Carson was known for his ability to find his way along Rocky Mountain trails. In 1838 he operated a trading post in what later became Kit Carson, Colorado.

Lon Chaney Sr. (1883–1930), from Colorado Springs, was an actor who starred in classic horror films, including *The Hunchback of Notre Dame* and *The Phantom of the Opera*. Because he wore a lot of makeup to change his appearance for each new role, he became known as the Man of a Thousand Faces.

Lon Chaney Sr.

Adolph Coors (1847–1919) moved from Germany to Golden, Colorado, and opened the Adolph Coors Company in 1880. This company has grown to be the largest beer maker in Colorado.

Jack Dempsey (1895–1983), considered to be one of the best boxers of all time, grew up in Manassa, Colorado. Nicknamed the Manassa Mauler, Dempsey held the title of heavyweight boxing champion for 16 years.

John Denver (1943–1997) was a musician who was born in New Mexico as Henry John Deutschendorf Jr. He later changed his name to John Denver and made his home in Colorado. The singer and songwriter gained international fame with popular songs such as "Rocky Mountain High" and "Sunshine on My Shoulders." He was named Colorado's poet laureate in 1974.

Mary Letha Elting (born 1906), an author from Creede, Colorado, has written several children's books, including *Wheels and Noises* and *The Answer Book*.

Carrie Jane Everson (1842–1914) was a scientist who moved from Chicago to Denver, where she became interested in mining practices in the 1870s. In her experiments with ground-up gold ore, she discovered a way to separate the precious metal from its ore. But it wasn't until after her death that she received credit for her accomplishment, called oil flotation, which eventually became a common method for separating metal from ore.

Douglas Fairbanks Sr. (1883–1939) starred in many adventure movies in the 1920s. Two of his most famous films are *The Three Musketeers* and *Robin Hood*. Fairbanks, who grew up in Denver, cofounded the United Artists film studio in 1919.

Adolph Coors

Jack Dempsey

John Denver

Douglas Fairbanks Sr.

Justina Ford

Ouray

David Packard

Federico Peña

Eugene Field (1850–1895) was an editor of the *Denver Tribune* in the early 1880s. Field, who is best known for his children's poems, wrote *Little Boy Blue* and *Wynken, Blynken and Nod*.

Justina Ford (1871–1952), the first African American woman in Colorado to become a doctor, settled in Denver in 1902. During her 50-year career, she delivered at least 7,000 babies in the Denver area, mostly for poor women. Her former Denver residence houses the Black American West Museum and Heritage Center.

Ouray (1834–1880), a Ute Indian leader, was widely respected for his skill in settling disputes between white settlers and Indians. He kept peace between settlers and his people for many years. A county, a city, and a mountain in Colorado are all named after him.

David Packard (1912–1996) was an engineer and businessperson who, along with William Hewlett, founded the Hewlett-Packard Company in 1939. The partners invented and sold machinery, including equipment for bowling alleys, and later began making high-tech computers. Packard grew up in Pueblo, Colorado.

Federico Peña (born 1947) was Denver's mayor from 1983 to 1991. Peña, a Mexican American, served two terms in a city where the population is mostly Anglo. In 1993 U.S. president Bill Clinton named Peña to head the U.S. Department of Transportation, and in 1997 he named Peña to head the U.S. Department of Energy.

Antoinette Perry (1888–1946), nicknamed Tony, was a well-known actress and theater director of the early 1900s. The Tony Awards, given each year to recognize achievement in theater, are named after her. Perry was born in Denver.

Antoinette Perry

Florence Sabin (1871–1953), a world-famous doctor from Central City, Colorado, received many honors for her research on tuberculosis, a deadly disease that affects the lungs. In the 1930s, she tested people in the Denver area for tuberculosis, greatly reducing the number of deaths caused by the disease.

Florence Sabin

Patricia Schroeder (born 1940) was the first woman elected to represent Colorado in the U.S. Congress. She served in the U.S. House of Representatives for 24 years—longer than any other woman.

Robert J. Seiwald (born 1925) is an inventor from Fort Morgan, Colorado. With a Ph.D. in organic chemistry, Seiwald helped discover that antigens (bacteria and viruses) can be identified. This means that the correct antibodies can be released to help stop the antigens from spreading. His research is very important in the search for a cure for AIDS.

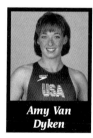

Amy Van Dyken

Amy Van Dyken (born 1973) is one of the world's top swimmers. At the 1996 Olympic Games in Atlanta, Georgia, Amy became the first American woman to win four gold medals at a single Olympic Games. She lives in Englewood, Colorado.

Byron R. White (born 1917) was an associate justice of the U.S. Supreme Court from 1962 to 1993. White graduated in 1938 from the University of Colorado, where he earned the nickname Whizzer for his skills on the football field. White is from Fort Collins, Colorado.

Byron White

FACTS-AT-A-GLANCE

Nickname: Centennial State

Song: "Where the Columbines Grow"

Motto: Nil sine Numine (Nothing Without the Deity)

Flower: white and lavender columbine

Tree: Colorado blue spruce

Bird: lark bunting

Animal: Rocky Mountain bighorn sheep

Insect: Colorado hairstreak butterfly

Fish: greenback cutthroat trout

Fossil: stegosaurus

Date and ranking of statehood: August 1, 1876, the 38th state

Capital: Denver

Area: 103,729 square miles

Rank in area, nationwide: 8th

Average January temperature: 28° F

Average July temperature: 74° F

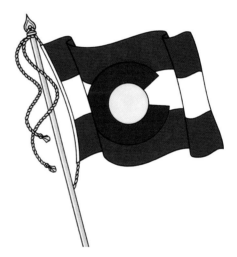

The red "C" on Colorado's flag stands for the name of the state and the reddish Colorado River. The gold circle in the center symbolizes mineral wealth. Colorado's blue skies and snowy mountains are represented by the blue and white stripes.

POPULATION GROWTH

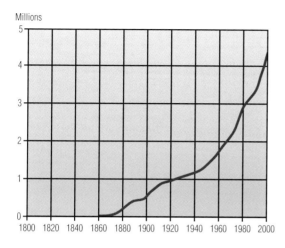

Millions

This chart shows how Colorado's population has grown from 1860 to 2000.

Colorado's seal includes a hammer and pick to represent mining and mountains to signify the rugged land. The triangular figure on top symbolizes the eye of God that is "all-seeing."

Population: 4,301,261 (2000 census)

Rank in population, nationwide: 24th

Major cities and populations: (2000 census) Denver (554,636), Colorado Springs (360,890), Aurora (276,393), Lakewood (144,126), Fort Collins (118,652)

U.S. senators: 2

U.S. representatives: 7

Electoral votes: 9

Natural resources: coal, fertile soil, gold, gravel, natural gas, oil, sand and stone

Agricultural products: beans, beef, corn, hay, lamb, milk, onions, potatoes, sugar beets, wheat

Manufactured goods: animal feed, beer, computers, electrical equipment, luggage, printed materials, scientific instruments, sporting goods

WHERE COLORADANS WORK

Services—67 percent (services includes jobs in trade; community, social, and personal services; finance, insurance, and real estate; transportation, communication, and utilities)

Government—14 percent

Manufacturing—8 percent

Construction—7 percent

Agriculture and fishing—3 percent

Mining—1 percent

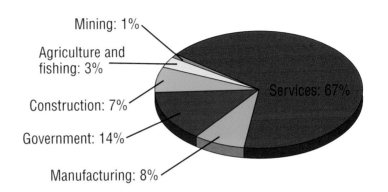

GROSS STATE PRODUCT

Services—66 percent

Government—13 percent

Manufacturing—12 percent

Construction—5 percent

Agriculture and fishing—2 percent

Mining—2 percent

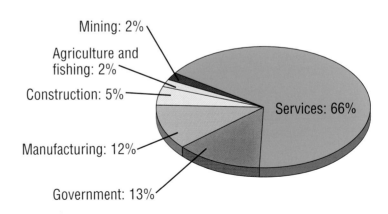

STATE WILDLIFE

Mammals: antelope, badger, bighorn sheep, black bear, coyote, deer, elk, fox, jackrabbit, moose, mountain lion, mule deer, wild horse

Birds: blue jay, grouse, lark bunting, mourning dove, peregrine falcon, pheasant, quail

Reptiles and amphibians: bullfrog, prairie lizard, rattlesnake, tiger salamander, western chorus frog, woodhouse's toad

Fish: bass, bluegill, catfish, crappie, perch, salmon, sunfish, trout

Trees: ash, aspen, cottonwood, fir, maple, pine, spruce

Wild plants: buffalo grass, buttercup, columbine, daisy, prickly pear cactus, violet, wild rose, yucca

Wildflowers on South Arapahoe Peak

PLACES TO VISIT

Bent's Old Fort National Historic Site, near La Junta
To experience what life was like for early American settlers in Colorado, visit this historic site. The fort was the state's first American settlement.

Boulder Museum of History
Housed in an 1899 mansion, this museum features exhibits on Colorado's past, especially the Boulder area.

Buffalo Bill's Grave, near Golden
William Cody, also known as Buffalo Bill, was a famous scout and showman of the American West. He is buried on top of Lookout Mountain.

Collage Children's Museum, Boulder
This museum for children features many hands-on exhibits about science, technology, literature, and other subjects.

Dinosaur National Monument, near Rangely
If you are fascinated by dinosaurs, then visit the Dinosaur National Monument. Fossils of dinosaur bones can be found in some of the park's large rock formations.

Durango & Silverton Narrow Gauge Railroad, Durango
Take a ride through the San Juan Mountains on this historic railroad, which remains completely coal fired and steam operated. It is the last passenger railroad of its kind in the United States. The railroad's museum is also in Durango.

Garden of the Gods, near Colorado Springs

It took millions of years for wind and rain to form the red sand-stone structures that make up this giant natural rock garden.

Mesa Verde National Park, near Cortez

A visit to this ancient historic site lets you travel back in time. Anasazi Indians lived in these cliff dwellings more than 700 years ago.

Museum of Western Art, Denver

The Museum of Western Art houses over 125 paintings and sculptures that depict scenes of the West.

Pikes Peak, near Colorado Springs

Pikes Peak, site of the 1858 gold rush, is one of the most famous mountains in the Rockies.

U.S. Mint, Denver

Have you ever wondered how money is made? Take a tour of the U.S. Mint, which produces millions of new coins each year. (Look on any U.S. coin, and you might see a tiny "D" near the date to show that it was made here.)

ANNUAL EVENTS

National Western Stock Show, Denver—*January*

World Cup Ski Racing Competitions, Vail and Aspen—*February and March*

Iron Horse Bicycle Classic, Durango—*May*

Ute Mountain Bear Dance, Towaoc—*June*

Strings in the Mountains Chamber Music Festival, Steamboat Springs—*July*

Festival of the Arts, Crested Butte—*August*

Aspen Leaf Tours, Cripple Creek—*September*

Rocky Mountain Colorfest, throughout southwestern Colorado—*September and October*

Parade of Lights, Denver—*December*

LEARN MORE ABOUT COLORADO

BOOKS

General

Ayer, Eleanor H. *Colorado.* New York: Benchmark Books, 1997. For older readers.

Fradin, Dennis Brindell. *Colorado.* Chicago: Children's Press, 1993.

Krudwig, Vickie Leigh. *Hiking Through Colorado History.* Englewood, CO: Westcliffe Publishers, 1998.

Wills, Charles A. *A Historical Album of Colorado.* Brookfield, CT: Millbrook Press, 1996.

Special Interest

Goodman, Susan E. *Stones, Bones, and Petroglyphs: Digging into Southwest Archaeology.* New York: Atheneum Books, 1998. Goodman takes readers on an archaeological field trip at the Crow Canyon Archaeological Center in Colorado.

Italia, Bob and Paul Joseph. *Colorado Rockies.* Minneapolis: ABDO Publishing Co., 1997. Part of the America's Game series, this book is filled with photographs and information about Denver's baseball team.

Lowry, Lois. *Aunt Clara Brown: Official Pioneer.* Minneapolis: Carolrhoda Books, Inc., 1999. This illustrated biography tells the story of a freed slave who made her fortune in Colorado and used the money to help other former slaves begin new lives.

Ross, Michael Elsohn. *Exploring the Earth with John Wesley Powell.* Minneapolis: Carolrhoda Books, Inc., 2000. This biography follows the life of John Wesley Powell, who explored the Colorado River and Grand Canyon. It also includes scientific information and activities for the budding naturalist.

Young, Mary Taylor. *On the Trail of Colorado Critters: Wildlife-Watching for Kids.* Denver: Denver Museum of Natural History Press, 2000. Over 60 of Colorado's creatures are featured in this engaging guidebook, which takes readers on an exploration of the state's wildlife.

Fiction

Lawlor, Laurie. *Gold in the Hills.* New York: Walker & Company, 1995. In this novel, ten-year-old Hattie and her brother, Pheme, try to make the best of their lives with a difficult older cousin while their father searches for gold in the Colorado mountains.

WEBSITES

State of Colorado
<http://www.state.co.us/>
Colorado's official website includes information about the state's government, economy, communities, and education.

State of Colorado Kids' Page
<http://www.state.co.us/kids/index.hmtl>
This website for young people is full of information about Colorado, including the state's history, geography, environment, literature, government, and tourist attractions. There's even a section with questions and answers to help students complete school reports about the state.

The Official Site for Colorado Travel and Tourism
<http://www.colorado.com/>
For general information about activities and attractions throughout Colorado or for travel information about specific cities, visit this website.

The Denver Post Online
<http://www.denverpost.com/>
Read about current events in the online version of this popular Colorado newspaper.

PRONUNCIATION GUIDE

Anasazi (ahn-uh-SAHZ-ee)

Apache (uh-PACH-ee)

Arapaho (uh-RAP-uh-hoh)

Cheyenne (shy-AN)

Comanche (kuh-MAN-chee)

Kiowa (KY-uh-waw)

Mesa Verde (MAY-suh VUHRD-ee)

Navajo (NAV-uh-hoh)

Pueblo (PWEHB-loh)

Rio Grande (ree-oh GRAND) or (ree-oh GRAHN-day)

Santa Fe (sant-uh FAY)

South Platte (SOWTH PLAT)

Ute (YOOT)

GLOSSARY

Anglo: a white person of European, non-Hispanic descent. Anglo is a term used primarily in the Southwest.

bluff: a steep, high bank, or cliff, especially along a river

continental divide: a line of elevated land that determines the direction in which the rivers of a continent flow

drought: a long period of extreme dryness due to lack of rain or snow

immigrant: a person who moves into a foreign country and settles there

irrigation: a method of watering land by directing water through canals, ditches, pipes, or sprinklers

Latino: a person living in the United States who either came from or has ancestors from Latin America. Latin America includes Mexico and Central and South America.

mesa: an isolated hill with steep sides and a flat top

park: a flat valley between mountain ranges

pass: a low opening in a mountain range

plateau: a large, relatively flat area that stands above the surrounding land

reservation: public land set aside by the government to be used by Native Americans

treaty: an agreement between two or more groups, usually having to do with peace or trade

INDEX

PHOTO ACKNOWLEDGMENTS

© Galen Rowell/Corbis, cover (left) © Dave G. Houser/Corbis, cover (right) PresentationMaps.com, pp. 1, 8, 9, 44; © Dave G. Houser/Corbis, pp., 2-3; © Buddy Mays/Corbis, p. 3; © Kent & Donna Dannen, pp. 4 (detail), 6, 7 (detail), 10, 12, 15 (top right, bottom right), 17 (detail), 22, 39 (detail), 43, 47, 49, 52 (both), 60, 73, 80; Sara Bledsoe, p. 11; R. E. Barber © 1991, p. 13; Jerry Hennen, pp. 14, 46 (top left, bottom); Lynda Richards, p. 15 (left); Karelle Scharff, p. 16 (both), 42, 45, 75; Museum of Western Colorado, p. 17 (Al Look Collection 191.115-775), 32 (Palisade Library Collection, 1972.23-65), 33 (Grand Valley Water Users Collection, 1980.115), 35 (William Chenoweth Collection, 1987.53), 36 (Frank Dean Photo, Al Look Collection, 2Ha57e); Frederica Georgia, p. 18; All rights reserved, Photo Archives, Denver Museum of Natural History, p. 19; Denver Public Library, Western History Department, pp. 21 (top) and 21 (bottom- L. Maynard Dixon), 23, 24, 28 (Arthur Shay), 29, 31 (left), 67 (top), 69 (top); Colorado Historical Society, p. 26 (Alex Comparet), 27 (Robert Lindneaux), 30 (F1780), 31 (right), 66 (top- F8098); Library of Congress, p. 34; © Chase Swift/Corbis, p. 37; © David Muench/Corbis, p. 38; Paul A. Pavlik, p. 40; © The Purcell Team/Corbis, p. 41; Saul Mayer, p. 46 (top right); U. S. Air Force Academy, p.48; © AFP/Corbis, p. 50; Colorado Tourism Board, pp. 51 (Jeff Andrew), 58 (Rod Walker); Herbert Fristedt, p. 53; © Ted Spiegel/Corbis, p. 54; United Airlines, p. 55; Colorado Department of Health, pp. 56, 69 (second from top); George Karn, p. 61; Tim Seeley, p. 63; NASA, p. 66 (second from top); Starsmore Center for Local History, Colorado Springs Pioneers Museum, p. 66 (second from bottom); Wisconsin Center for Film and Theater Research, p. 66 (bottom); Independent Picture Service, pp. 67 (second from top), 68 (second from top, bottom), 69 (bottom); © Lynn Goldsmith/Corbis, p. 67 (second from bottom); Hollywood Book and Poster Company, p. 67 (bottom); Black American West Museum and Heritage Center, p. 68 (top); Hewlett Packard, p. 68 (second from bottom); © Allsport USA/ Simon Bruty, p. 69 (second from bottom).